Peace of
Mind®

Peace of Mind
Flex Curriculum

Grades 1 & 2

Fifteen engaging flexible lessons that equip students with
the skills to manage big emotions, build healthy relationships,
solve conflicts peacefully, and express feelings in
American Sign Language

Linda Ryden
Including original stories, illustrations and videos

Welcome to the Peace of Mind Community!

Questions? Comments?
We'd love to hear from you!

Please visit teachpeaceofmind.org or contact us at info@TeachPeaceofMind.org.

Peace of Mind Publications

Curriculum

Peace of Mind Core Curriculum for Early Childhood
Peace of Mind Core Curriculum for Grades 1 & 2
Peace of Mind Core Curriculum for Grade 3
Peace of Mind Core Curriculum for Grades 4 & 5
Peace of Mind Core Curriculum for Middle School
Peace of Mind Flex Curriculum for Kindergarten
Peace of Mind Flex Curriculum for Grades 1 & 2
Peace of Mind Flex Curriculum for Grade 3
Peace of Mind Flex Curriculum for Grade 4
Peace of Mind Flex Curriculum for Grades 5-8
Social Justice Lesson Curriculum for Grades 3-5

Storybooks

Henry is Kind
Rosie's Brain / El Cerebro de Rosita
Marleigh is Mindful / Marleigh practica la conciencia plena
Marleigh's Big Feelings
Mason and the Conflict CAT / Mason y el conflicto CAT
Quinn and the Worry Channel
Sergio Sees the Good
Tyaja Uses the Think Test

TeachPeaceofMind.org

Peace of Mind Inc. Washington DC 20015
https://TeachPeaceofMind.org
Copyright 2025 Linda Ryden and Peace of Mind Inc.

Editor: Cheryl Cole Dodwell
Cover and Interior Design: Schwa Design Group
Illustrations, Graphics and Videos: Linda Ryden
Logo: Pittny Creative
ISBN: 979-8-9998662-0-2
LCCN: 2025917679
Published 2025

Peace of Mind Flex Curriculum for Grades 1-2

Peace of Mind Flex At-a-Glance

Lesson	Topic	Mindfulness Practice and ASL	Materials Needed
All lessons require a way to show a short video to the class and your Kindness Pal list. Worksheets and Coloring Sheets are included with the lessons.			
1.	Introduction to Mindfulness and Kindness Pals	Four Square Breathing ASL: Happy	Four Square Breathing Coloring Sheet
2	Take Five Breathing	Four Square Breathing and Take Five Breathing ASL: Sad	Take Five Breathing Coloring Sheet and Worksheet
3	Gravity Hands	Gravity Hands and Four Square Breathing ASL: Angry	Gravity Hands Coloring Sheet
4	Squeeze and Release	Squeeze and Release and Gravity Hands ASL: Scared	Squeeze and Release Coloring Sheet
5	Flower Breathing	Flower Breathing and Squeeze and Release ASL: Silly	Flower Breath Coloring Sheet
6	Candle and Bubble Breathing	Candle and Bubble Breathing and Squeeze and Release ASL: Surprised	Candle Breathing Coloring Sheet & Bubble Worksheet
7	Visualization	Visualization and Candle Breathing ASL: Peaceful	Visualization Coloring Sheet
8	Gratefuls	Visualization and Gratitude Practice ASL: Worried	Gratitude Coloring Sheet and Gratefuls Worksheet
9	Make up Your own Breath	Mindfulness Helper Choice ASL: Loved	Create your Own Breath Worksheet
10	Sergio Sees the Good	Mindfulness Helper Choice ASL: I feel	Paper Cups, Marbles or Paper Clips
11	Rosie's Brain	Mindfulness Helper Choice ASL: Frustrated	Brain Poster Copies
12	Daisy and Cactus: What is a Conflict?	Mindfulness Helper Choice Today? ASL: Excited	–
13	Jack and Louise: Conflict Resolution Practice	Mindfulness Helper Choice ASL: How are you feeling	–
14	Henry is Kind	Heartfulness ASL: hungry	Heartfulness Worksheet
15	Kindness Chain	Heartfulness ASL: Thirsty	Just yourselves!

Introduction to the Peace of Mind Peace of Mind Flex Curriculum

Welcome to the Peace of Mind Flex Curriculum! If you are looking for a series of flexible mindfulness-based SEL lessons that can be used daily or weekly, this curriculum is for you! This Flex Curriculum is designed to be used in schools and out-of-school time programs where time or staffing constraints allow only 15-20 minutes for social and emotional learning lessons. Lessons may be broken up into modules and taught over the course of a week.

Curriculum Theory of Change

Our Theory of Change (ToC) is the same for both our Flex Curriculum and our Core Curriculum. The ToC includes our Curriculum Pillars, Learning Experiences, Core Teaching Practices, and the Outcomes we hope to see for students. Here it is:

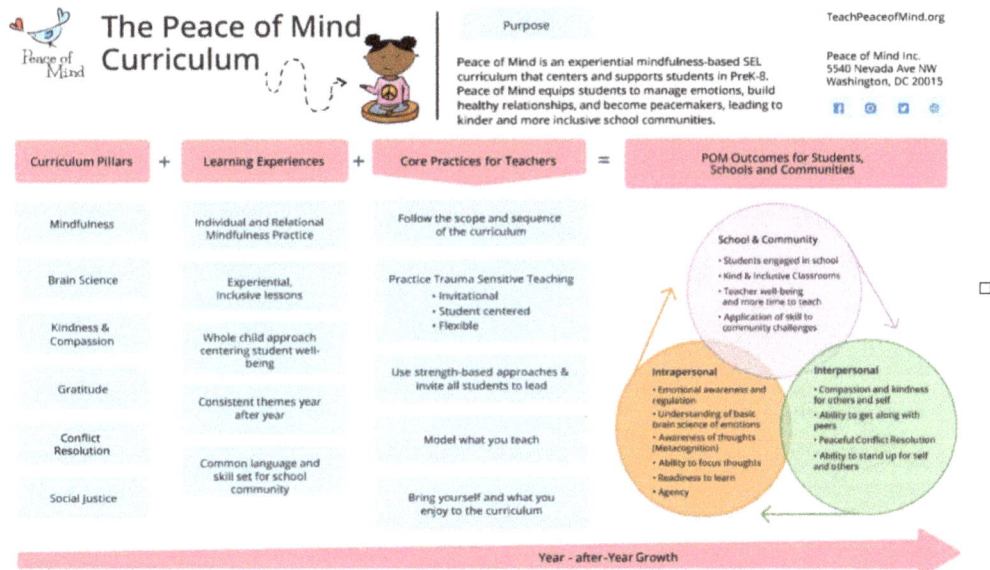

Pillars
The Flex Curriculum is built on Peace of Mind's 6 foundational pillars: Mindfulness, Brain Science, Kindness and Compassion, Gratitude, Conflict Resolution and Social Justice. Engaging and fun, this mini-series uses animated stories and mindfulness practice videos along with interactive discussions and activities to engage students in:

- experiencing mindfulness practice for themselves;
- learning what happens in their brains when they experience a big emotion;

- learning how mindful practices can affect their ability to respond;
- learning how mindfulness can help in resolving conflicts peacefully.

Every lesson ends with Kindness Pals, a pair practice that helps students get to know each other and build a caring classroom community in a relatively short time.

Learning Experiences

This Flex Curriculum, like our Core Curriculum, is designed to promote learning experiences that center student well-being and agency while supporting a kind and inclusive classroom and school community. You'll notice that students learn mindfulness not only for themselves, but for their relationships with others. The curriculum is experiential and inclusive with opportunities for student leadership and personal growth throughout. Schools that use Peace of Mind year-after-year in all grade levels will find consistent themes with age-appropriate lessons. Peace of Mind also helps school communities to develop a common language and skill set related to our own well-being, building healthy relationships, and solving conflicts peacefully.

Outcomes

When taught with fidelity, The Peace of Mind Flex Curriculum will help students to:

- Increase their self-awareness and self-regulation;
- Understand the basic science related to their emotions;
- Regularly practice kindness, compassion and gratitude;
- Be more aware of and more skillfully focus their thoughts;
- Build positive relationships with peers and adults;
- Build kind and inclusive classrooms.

Core Teaching Practices

Through our work with partner schools and academic researchers, we have identified five core teaching practices for effective, impactful implementation of Peace of Mind.

1. **Follow the Scope and Sequence of the Curriculum**

   The Flex Curriculum is built around the first 5 pillars detailed below. This lesson sequence is designed to first give students a foundational set of mindfulness practices to help them manage their emotions and learn to put space between their reactions to a big feeling and their response. Gratitude practice follows and an introduction to one aspect of how our brains work: our negativity bias. Students learn more basic brain science in the lesson on Rosie's Brain. The curriculum, like every lesson, closes with

kindness practice. With this foundation, students are ready for the conflict resolution lessons.

- **Mindfulness**
  In all lessons, students learn and practice mindfulness exercises, building their own tool kit to help them notice and manage big emotions. Students experience the effects of each practice personally and begin to discern which practices are most helpful to them.

- **Gratitude**
  We explore gratitude in several different ways including our brain's tendency to focus on the negative and how gratitude practice helps to balance this tendency by focusing on small good things we experience. Through stories, games and activities, students experience this for themselves.

- **Brain Science**
  Through the Rosie's Brain story, students gain powerful insight into what happens in our brains when we get angry and why mindfulness helps us calm down.

- **Conflict Resolution**
  Building on the foundation laid in earlier lessons, students learn to use mindfulness and a new understanding of their brains to understand when they are in a conflict and how they can use their skills to calm down, apologize and work out a peaceful solution.

- **Kindness and Compassion**
  We end the curriculum with a focus on self-compassion and compassion for others, making a Kindness Chain as a final way of connecting with and appreciating each other.

- **Social Justice**
  Former U.S. Surgeon General Vivek Murthy said that "mental health is the defining public health crisis of our time." The ultimate goal of the Peace of Mind Program is to create a kinder, more peaceful world with and for our children. We begin by helping to create classroom communities where students feel loved and seen. We help children and their grownups learn how to recognize and manage their emotions, how to feel compassion for others and themselves and how to work out conflicts peacefully. We hope that with these personal and interpersonal skills, children will grow up to find peaceful solutions to the most challenging social justice issues of our time.

2. Practice Trauma Sensitive Teaching

You will notice in the lesson scripts three important components of trauma-sensitive teaching:

- **Invitational** - Mindfulness practice is always invitational. While we expect everyone to sit together during the mindful moments, we invite students to choose whether or not to engage with a practice. They can choose for themselves, but they cannot interfere with someone else's choice. We ask everyone to be respectful of others while making their own decision about whether to do a practice or not. Students are welcome to just sit quietly.

- **Student-centered** - We teach mindfulness practices for students' own well-being. We teach a variety of practices not so students can master them all, but so they can find the ones that work best for them. If a student is having a hard time with a practice, suggest that they choose another one that works better for them.

- **Flexible** - We don't require students to close their eyes or sit in a certain way to practice. If students need to make modifications to a practice (keeping their eyes open or walking quietly in the back of the room, for example) to help themselves feel comfortable this is fine as long as their choices do not interfere with others' comfort and safety.

3. Use Strength-Based Approaches

You will notice that the scripts offered for the lessons use strength-based language: language that focuses on students' abilities, interests and potential, not deficits. The curriculum is designed to promote student agency and leadership, especially through the role of Mindfulness Helper. The Mindfulness Helper is a student who leads the class in the mindfulness practice for the day. Here's how it works:

- The teacher consults their alphabetical roll list and chooses a student to be the Mindfulness Helper (MH) for the day.

- The teacher encourages the class to offer sign language applause for the person who is chosen that day.

- The MH can sit near the teacher.

- With the teacher's help the MH says slowly, "Let's get into our mindful bodies…. Let's close our eyes or look down. … Let's Invite three deep breaths." Always offer the students a choice about keeping their eyes open or closed. At this point the teacher will lead the rest of the mindfulness practice as instructed in the lesson.

- The MH rings the bell/chime when the mindfulness practice is complete.
- The teacher then asks the MH to return to their seat.
- You will need to help students remember what to say at the beginning of the year. Repeating the same words each class is important to help students develop a routine to help them begin to practice on their own.

  Read more about this on Page 9 of the Core Curriculum for Grades 1&2.

4. **Model What You Teach**

   We know from research and our own experience that modeling what we are teaching is one of the most effective ways of engaging our students in mindfulness practice themselves. Students Invite their cues from you. You don't have to be an expert in mindfulness, but it is important to join your students on the journey.

   Read more about this on Page 12 of the Core Curriculum.

5. **Bring Yourself to the Curriculum**

   Once you are comfortable with the first four core teaching practices, we hope you will be able to bring yourself to the curriculum. If the script isn't quite how you would say things, please adapt so you feel comfortable. If you enjoy singing, bring that in! If you enjoy crafts, make that a part of what you do. If puppets are your thing, they're welcome!

Setting Expectations

The *Peace of Mind* curriculum plants seeds of mindfulness and compassion. These seeds grow and mature inside a student's mind and heart, positively affecting the way a person sees the world and operates within it. For some students, the outward positive effects are manifested quickly and clearly. For other students, it may take more time, and the outward signs of change may be subtle. All that we expect of students is to try to practice the skills in this curriculum as often as they can —just to try.

Some students have a much easier time sitting quietly than others. Keep your expectations reasonable. Sometimes a student who is sitting with their eyes wide open, legs jiggling, and fiddling with a pencil—but not talking—during mindfulness practice is doing their very best and is benefiting greatly from the effort. That's okay. The exercises in this curriculum are for the benefit of the children and, as long as they are not preventing other children from practicing, a little wiggling around is okay.

Try to put the guidelines in positive language such as "As long as you follow the directions you can continue to play the game." This can be much more effective than the more traditional way of saying, "If you don't follow the rules you can't play." Many children react negatively to orders like that but are perfectly happy to follow the rules when they are stated in a more neutral way.

Materials Needed

- **Lesson** Slides. Accessible through QR code here:

- **Storybooks**

  Marleigh is Mindful, Sergio Sees the Good, Rosie's Brain and *Henry is Kind* either in print copies or video read-alouds (links included in lessons).

- **Worksheet and Coloring Sheet Copies**

  You will find related coloring sheets and worksheets right after each lesson. Please print what you need for your class. See "At-A-Glance" to easily find what you need for each lesson.

  Here's an idea! Send coloring sheets home after each class so that parents know what their children are learning in Peace Class. Or, turn the Coloring Sheets into a book for your students to Invite home at the end of the session!

- **Chime (optional)**

A Note About American Sign Language

A new addition to the Peace of Mind Curriculum, American Sign Language is a wonderful tool to use to help all children, regardless of English proficiency, learn about, explore and communicate their emotions. These lessons offer a very basic introduction to expressing emotions in American Sign Language. The ASL included here is just an introduction to a rich language that can be used to communicate with students who are deaf and hard of hearing or who have other communication challenges.

For more information about learning ASL please visit:
www.nad.org/resources/american-sign-language/
learning-american-sign-language

A Note on Kindness Pals

Kindness Pals is an engaging and powerful activity that takes place every class period. Kindness Pal practice reminds children to make kindness part of their daily lives. Doing kind things for their Kindness Pals spills over into their treatment of others and so they can develop the habit of treating people with kindness through regular practice. Kindness Pals also gives children opportunities to get to know each other and to connect with others whom they might not have gotten along with in the past or whom they think they just don't like. Here's a quick video introduction to Kindness Pals.

Here is how it works:

- For each class, assign each student one Kindness Pal. You can pair up children in advance to ensure there aren't any repeated partnerships.

- When each child hears their Kindness Pal's name, emphasize that both pals, or the whole class, must say "Okay." **This is very important.** This response lets the teacher know that they have heard their assignment and that they know who their Kindness Pal is. Please practice this routine with your class. (**Watch this video** of kids doing Kindness pals.)

- Please let the class know that this is not a time for them to let the teacher or the class know how they feel about having that Kindness Pal. This avoids hurt feelings and also offers multiple chances to remind the children that they have the power to be kind and the power to hurt people's feelings. It all depends on their choices. This is a powerful lesson.

- Explain to the students that they will each receive one Kindness Pal each class period (or each week if you choose). Kindness Pals will participate in an activity together during the class period.

- You may also invite the students to do small kind things for their assigned Kindness Pals before the next class. Some examples of kind behavior might be to get a Pal's snack, stack their chair, or play together at recess. The following class, allow a few minutes for children to talk about what they did for their Pal.

- Kindness Pals sharing time is a perfect time to practice mindful listening. It's important to demonstrate how we listen mindfully with our whole bodies. You might even want to let a student lead the sharing.

- Assign new pals at the end of each class (or week).

Lesson 1
Introduction to Mindfulness and Kindness Pals

Slides 1-12

1. **Welcome** to Peace of Mind!

   We're going to be learning about something called mindfulness. Have you ever heard of mindfulness before? What do you think it means? **Invite some answers.**

   Mindfulness means to pay attention, and we can pay attention to many different things. Mindfulness can also be about using our breath to help us Invite care of ourselves. How do you breathe when you run around for a long time? How do you breathe when you are scared? How do you breathe when you are nervous?

   Today we are going to watch a video about a girl named Marleigh who we will be getting to know in Peace of Mind Class. She's a really good dancer, but she gets nervous when she has to perform in front of an audience. Do you ever get nervous? Let's see what Marleigh does when she gets nervous.

2. **Mindful Moment**

   Show Marleigh Four Square Video Marleigh introduces mindfulness and teaches the first practice.

   Try Four Square Breathing with the class.

   Try taking 3 breaths this way.

3. **American Sign Language (ASL)**

   AUTHOR'S NOTE: A new addition to the Peace of Mind Curriculum, American Sign Language is a wonderful tool to use to help all children, regardless of English proficiency, learn about, explore and communicate their emotions. These lessons offer a very basic, simple introduction to expressing emotions in American Sign Language. The ASL included here is just an introduction to a rich language that can be used to communicate with students who are deaf and hard of hearing or who have other communication challenges. For more information about learning ASL please visit: https://www.nad.org/resources/american-sign-language/learning-american-sign-language/

Discuss: *Does breathing this way make you feel any different? Is it hard to hold your breath? Can you do it gently? Why do you think Four Square Breathing helped Marleigh feel less nervous about her performance? How do you feel?*

American Sign Language (ASL)
You might say: *We're going to be learning a new way to share our feelings with each other called American Sign Language or ASL. ASL is a visual language - a language that we see with our eyes instead of listening to with our ears.*

When we use ASL, we use our facial expressions, hand signals and body movements instead of saying words with our voices. Most of the people who use ASL are deaf (which means that they cannot hear with their ears) or hard of hearing which means they have trouble hearing with their ears. But lots of other people use it too. Once we learn how to share our feelings in ASL we'll start using it to share our feelings with each other.

We're going to start out by learning how to say "Happy. "
How do you feel in your body when you are happy?

Choose a few volunteers to demonstrate what "happy" looks like.
Let's watch a video of one of the Peace of Mind students showing us how to sign "Happy. " **Happy Video (the video is in the slides)**

4. Kindness Pals

Introduce Kindness Pals
Now we're going to do something fun called Kindness Pals. Every class we're going to get a new Kindness Pal. Your Kindness Pal is somebody that you will get to know a little bit better. You get to do kind things for them, and they get to do kind things for you. Then, next time you'll get a new Kindness Pal. There's one important rule of Kindness Pals. When I tell you who your Kindness Pal is I want you to say, 'Okay!' in a nice friendly way. Let's try that together!

Are you always going to feel really excited about who you got? Maybe not. And that's okay. But how do you think we will make our Kindness pal feel if we say, 'Aw!' or, 'Rats!' or, 'But I wanted Lily!' That's right, they'll feel really bad. Since this is your Kindness Pal it's your job to be kind to them - just for one day. So, the first kind thing you're going to do for them is to say, "Okay!"

*Let's **watch** a quick video of some students about Kindness Pals and having fun with them.*

Assign Kindness Pals

Remind the students to say, "Okay!". You can make a list ahead of time or put their names on popsicle sticks and pull them randomly out of a jar. However you want to do them is fine. Just make sure that they get a different child each time and that they say, "Okay!"

Kindness Pal Activity

Now we're going to do an activity with your Kindness Pal. When I say "Go!" you're going to find your Kindness Pal and then I'm going to give you 30 seconds to find out how many things you have in common - how many things are the same about you. You can ask each other about foods you like, animals, colors, books, movies, toys, whatever!

Share what they have in common.
Who thinks they have the most things in common? Have everyone share one thing that they had in common with their Kindness Pal.

Now for the rest of the day see if you can find any more things you have in common and try to do some kind things for your Kindness Pal.

5. Optional

Four Square Breathing Coloring Sheet (follows lesson)

6. Closing

Let's take a moment to think about something kind you could do for your Kindness Pal today. You can close your eyes if you want to.
Wait.
Ask: *Who has an idea already of what you might do?* **Invite a few answers.**
You might say: *Thanks for a great class, everyone!*
Ring a bell or chime if you have one.

Extension: *Peace of Mind Core Curriculum* Lesson 1: Mindful Listening, page 22

Four Square Breathing

Lesson 2
Take Five Breathing

Slides 13-24

1. Introduction

From now on you will choose a student to be the Mindfulness Helper for each class. That student will come up front to sit or stand next to you and help you to lead a mindfulness practice. If you have a little bell or chime you can let the Mindfulness Helper ring it at the end of the mindfulness practice.

2. Mindful Moment

Review Four Square Breathing.
Ask if anybody remembers how to do Four Square Breathing.
Choose a Mindfulness Helper and ask them to lead it with your help.

Have the Mindfulness Helper say: _"Let's get into our mindful bodies. Let's close our eyes or look down_ (it's important _not_ to require students to close their eyes or sit in a particular way. As long as the students are not bothering each other they are fine). _Let's do Four Square Breathing."_

Then practice a few rounds of Four Square Breathing. Have the Mindfulness Helper ring a bell or chime if you have one - not necessary!

Learn a new mindfulness practice with Marleigh's little brother Mason called Take Five Breathing. **Watch the video.**

Try Take Five Breathing with the class

Discuss
Does breathing this way make you feel any different? Did Take Five Breathing help Mason? Have you ever been mad about having to clean up when you wanted to play? How could Take Five Breathing help you? How did it make you feel?

3. American Sign Language (ASL)

Today we're going to learn how to say "Sad" in ASL.
How do you feel in your body when you are sad?

Choose a few volunteers to demonstrate what "sad" looks like.

Let's watch a video of one of the Peace of Mind students showing us how to sign "sad." **(the video is in the slides)**

ASL Practice
Have everyone try to say "sad" in ASL. Point out that the sign for "sad" involves our faces, hand gestures and body motions. Ask them if the sign for "sad" matches the way that they feel when they are happy.

4. Kindness Pals

Assign New Kindness Pals
You can make a list ahead of time, or put their names on popsicle sticks and pull them randomly out of a jar, however you want to do them is fine. Just make sure that they get a different child each time and that they say "Okay!"

You might say: *Remember, every class we're going to get a new Kindness Pal. Your Kindness Pal is somebody that you will get to know a little bit better and you get to do kind things for them. Then next time you'll get a new Kindness Pal. There's one important rule of Kindness Pals. Does anybody remember what it is? When I tell you who your Kindness Pal is I want you to say "Okay!" in a nice friendly way.*

Kindness Pal Activity
Now we're going to do an activity with your Kindness Pal. When I say "Go!" you're going to find your Kindness Pal and you're going to play the Mirror Game.

We're going to be moving mindfully and really focusing on what our Kindness Pal is doing. What do you think it means to move mindfully? **Invite a few answers.**

Moving mindfully just means to really pay attention to how your body is moving.

Here's how to play the Mirror Game.
Choose a volunteer to demonstrate the Mirror Game with you.

You are going to take turns being the leader and doing slow movements with your body. Your Kindness Pal will try to be your reflection in the mirror and do

*the exact same movements. After one minute I will ask you to switch and the
other person will be the leader.*

5. Optional drawing activities

- Take Five Breathing Coloring Sheet (follows lesson)
- Trace your hand and decorate it to help you remember how to do Take
Five Breathing.(worksheet follows lesson)

6. Closing

*Let's take a moment to think about something kind you could do for your
Kindness pal today. You can close your eyes if you want to.*
Wait.
Ask: *Who has an idea already of what you might do?* **Invite a few answers.**
You might say: *Thanks for a great class, everyone!*
Ring a bell or chime if you have one.

Take Five Breathing

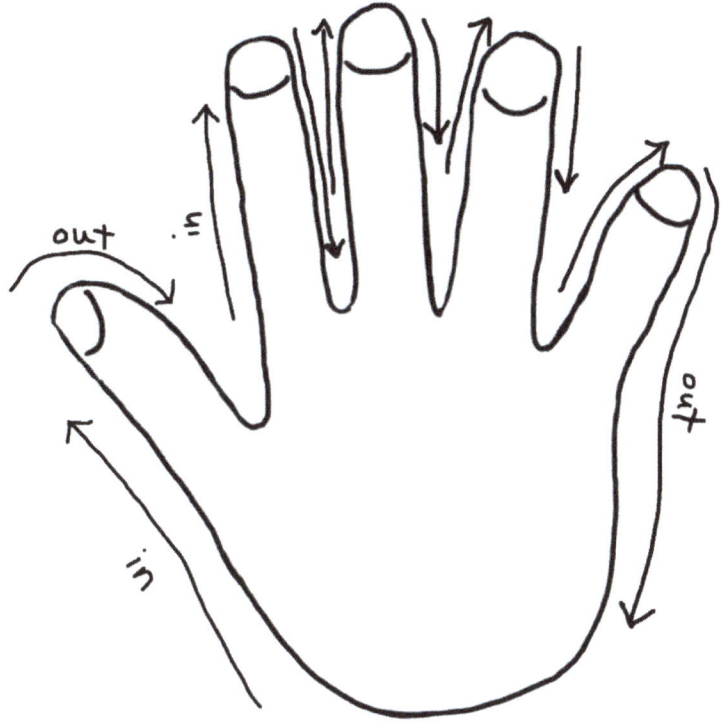

Slowly trace your hand breathing in as you
trace up and out as you trace down.

Take Five Breathing

Trace your hand and then decorate it to help you remember how to do Take Five Breathing.

Lesson 3
Gravity Hands

Slides 25-36

1. Introduction

You might say: Today we are going to learn another mindfulness practice and review the one we learned last time. We're also going to talk about our favorite things with our Kindness Pals.

2. Mindful Moment

Ask if anybody remembers how to do Take Five Breathing.

Choose the Mindfulness Helper and have them lead Take Five Breathing.

Remind the MH to say, *"Let's get into our mindful bodies. Let's close our eyes or look down* (it's important not to require students to close their eyes). *Let's do Take Five Breathing."*

Practice a few rounds of Take Five Breathing.

Ring a bell or chime (or let the Mindfulness Helper ring it) if you have one - not necessary!

Learn a new mindfulness practice with Navaneet called **Gravity Hands.**
Watch the video. **Try** Gravity Hands with the class.

Discuss

Does breathing this way make you feel any different? How did Gravity Hands help Navaneet? Why do you think we call it Gravity Hands?

3. American Sign Language (ASL)

Today we're going to learn how to say "Angry" in ASL.
How do you feel in your body when you are angry?

Choose a few volunteers to demonstrate what "angry" looks like.

Let's watch a video of one of the Peace of Mind students showing us how to sign "angry." **(the video is in the slides)**

ASL Practice

Have everyone try to say "angry" in ASL. Point out that the sign for "angry" involves our faces, hand gestures and body motions. Ask them if the sign for "angry" matches the way that they feel when they are angry.

Kindness Pals

Assign New *Kindness Pals: Okay it's time to get our new Kindness Pals! There's one important rule of Kindness Pals. Does anybody remember what it is? When I tell you who your Kindness Pal is I want you to say "Okay!" in a nice friendly way.*

Kindness Pal Activity

Okay when I say go you're going to find your Kindness Pal and you're going to talk about food! Ask each other what is one of your favorite things to eat for breakfast, lunch, dinner and dessert. You've got one minute! Go!

Share

Now you're going to vote with your feet. This corner is for people who like sweet foods the best. The other corner is for people who like salty foods the best. Ready? Go!

4. Optional

Gravity Hands Coloring Sheet (follows lesson)

5. Closing

Let's take a moment to think about something kind you could do for your Kindness pal today. You can close your eyes if you want to.
Wait.
Ask: *Who has an idea already of what you might do?* **Invite a few answers.**
You might say: *Thanks for a great class, everyone!*
Ring a bell or chime if you have one.

Extension: *Peace of Mind Core Curriculum for Grades 1 & 2: Lessons 10 and 12*

Gravity Hands

Slowly move your hands up
and down as you breathe in
and out.

Lesson 4
Squeeze and Release

Slides 37-47

1. Introduction

You might say:*Today we are going to learn another mindfulness practice and review the one we learned last time. We're going to spend some time with our new Kindness Pal finding out what we have in common.*

2. Mindful Moment

Choose the Mindfulness Helper and Review

Ask if anybody remembers how to do Gravity Hands.

Choose the Mindfulness Helper and have them lead Gravity Hands.

Remind them to say, *"Let's get into our mindful bodies. Let's close our eyes or look down* (it's important not to require students to close their eyes*). Let's do Gravity Hands."* **Practice** a few rounds of Gravity Hands.

Ring a bell or chime if you have one - not necessary!

Ask if anybody remembers how to do Four Square Breathing. Choose someone to demonstrate. Have somebody demonstrate Take Five Breathing.

Learn a new mindfulness practice with August called **Squeeze and Release.**

Watch the video. **Try** Squeeze and Release with the class.

Discuss

Does squeezing and releasing your body this way make you feel any differently? How did Squeeze and Release help August?

3. American Sign Language (ASL)

Today we're going to learn how to say "Scared" in ASL.
How do you feel in your body when you feel scared?

Choose a few volunteers to demonstrate what "scared" looks like.

Let's watch a video of one of the Peace of Mind students showing us how to sign "scared." **(the video is in the slides)**

ASL Practice

Have everyone try to say "scared" in ASL. Point out that the sign for scared involves our faces, hand gestures and body motions. Ask them if the sign for scared matches the way that they feel when they are scared .

4. Kindness Pals

Assign New Kindness Pals

Remind the students to say "Okay!" and make sure everyone is getting someone new today.

You might say: *Okay it's time to get our new Kindness Pals! There's one important rule of Kindness Pals. Does anybody remember what it is? When I tell you who your Kindness Pal is I want you to say "Okay!" in a nice friendly way.*

Kindness Pal Activity

Now we're going to do an activity with your Kindness Pal. When I say "Go!" you're going to find your Kindness Pal and then I'm going to give you 30 seconds to find out how many things you have in common - how many things are the same about you. You can ask each other about foods you like, animals, colors, books, movies, toys, whatever!

Share

Who thinks they have the most things in common? Have everyone share one thing that they had in common with their Kindness Pal. *Now for the rest of the day see if you can find any kind things to do for your Kindness Pal.*

5. Optional

Squeeze and Release Coloring Sheet (follows lesson)

6. Closing

Let's take a moment to think about something kind you could do for your Kindness pal today. You can close your eyes if you want to.

Wait.

Ask: *Who has an idea already of what you might do?* **Invite a few answers.**

You might say: *Thanks for a great class, everyone!* **Ring** a bell or chime if you have one.

Squeeze and Release

Slowly squeeze and
release parts of your body
as you breathe in and out

Lesson 5
Flower Breathing

Slides 48-57

1. Introduction

You might say: *Today we are going to learn another mindfulness practice and review the one we learned last time. We're going to spend some time with our new Kindness Pal finding out what we have in common.*

2. Mindful Moment

Choose the Mindfulness Helper and Review

Ask if anybody remembers how to do Squeeze and Release.

Choose the Mindfulness Helper and have them lead Squeeze and Release.

Remind them to say, *Let's get into our mindful bodies. Let's close our eyes or look down* (it's important not to require students to close their eyes). *Let's do* Squeeze and Release.

Practice a few rounds of Squeeze and Release.

Ring a bell or chime if you have one.

Ask if anybody remembers how to do the other practices you've been learning. Ask them to demonstrate briefly.

Learn a new mindfulness practice with Josie and Cybbie called **Flower Breathing. Watch the video. Try** Flower Breathing with the class.

Discuss

How does Flower Breathing make you feel? How did Flower Breathing help Josie?

3. American Sign Language (ASL)

Today we're going to learn how to say "Silly" in ASL.
How do you feel in your body when you feel silly?

Choose a few volunteers to demonstrate what "silly" looks like.

Let's watch a video of one of the Peace of Mind students showing us how to sign "silly." **(the video is in the slides)**

ASL Practice

Have everyone try to say "silly" in ASL. Point out that the sign involves our faces, hand gestures and body motions. Ask them if the sign matches the way that they feel when they feel silly.

4. Kindness Pals

Assign New *Kindness Pals:* **Remind** the students to say "Okay!" and make sure everyone is getting someone new today.

You might say: *It's time to get our new Kindness Pals! There's one important rule of Kindness Pals. Does anybody remember what it is? When I tell you who your Kindness Pal is, I want you to say "Okay!" in a nice friendly way.*

Kindness Pal Activity -

When I say go, you're going to find your Kindness Pal and play Switcheroo!
Choose a volunteer to model how to play the game.
You might say: *You and your partner will observe each other for one minute, then turn your backs to each other and switch one thing. Turn around and take turns guessing what has changed about their partner. Ready? Go!*
Ideas: Change your hair a little bit, roll down or up your sleeve, untie your shoe, pull up your sock. If they seem ready, you can up the challenge by changing **two** things.

5. Optional

Flower Breathing Coloring Sheet (follows lesson)

6. Closing

Let's take a moment to think about something kind you could do for your Kindness pal today. You can close your eyes if you want to.
Wait.
Ask: *Who has an idea already of what you might do?* **Invite a few answers.**
You might say: *Thanks for a great class, everyone!*
Ring a bell or chime if you have one.

———————————

Extensions: Peace of Mind Core Curriculum for Grades 1 & 2: Lesson 5: Mindful Seeing p. 41

Flower Breaths

Imagine you have a flower.
Smell the flower for four counts.
Blow the petals for four counts.

Lesson 6
Candle and Bubble Breathing

Slides 59-71

1. Introduction

You might say: *Today we are going to learn a new mindfulness practice and review the one we learned last time. We'll talk with our Kindness Pals about our favorite practices.*

2. Mindful Moment

Choose the Mindfulness Helper and Review

Ask if anybody remembers how to do Flower Breathing.

Choose the Mindfulness Helper and have them lead Flower Breathing.

Remind them to say, *"Let's get into our mindful bodies. Let's close our eyes or look down* (it's important not to require students to close their eyes). *Let's do Flower Breathing."*

Practice a few rounds of Flower Breathing.

Ring a bell or chime if you have one.

Ask if anybody remembers how to do the other practices you've been learning. Ask them to demonstrate briefly.

Learn two new mindfulness practices with Zivana and Persida called Candle Breathing and Bubble Breathing. **Watch the video. Try** Candle Breathing with the class.

Discuss: *How does Candle Breathing make you feel? How did Candle Breathing help Zivana?*

Try Bubble Breathing with the class.

Discuss: *How does Bubble Breathing make you feel? How did Bubble Breathing help Persida?*

3. American Sign Language (ASL)

Today we're going to learn how to say "Surprised" in ASL.
How do you feel in your body when you feel surprised?

Choose a few volunteers to demonstrate what "surprised" looks like.

Let's watch a video of one of the Peace of Mind students showing us how to sign "surprised" **(the video is in the slides)**

ASL Practice
Have everyone try to say "surprised" in ASL. Point out that the sign involves our faces, hand gestures and body motions. Ask them if the sign matches the way that they feel when they feel silly.

4. Kindness Pals

Assign New Kindness Pals: *Okay it's time to get our new Kindness Pals! There's one important rule of Kindness Pals. Does anybody remember what it is? When I tell you who your Kindness Pal is I want you to say "Okay!" in a nice friendly way.*

Kindness Pal Activity: *Okay when I say go you're going to find your Kindness Pal and tell each other what your favorite mindfulness practice is so far and ask each other why you like that one the best.*

Share: Vote with your feet: Label sections of the room for each mindfulness practice we've learned so far and ask them to go stand with the one they like the best. If there's time you can do their second favorite, third favorite, etc.

5. Optional

Candle Breathing Coloring Sheet and Bubble Breathing Drawing Sheet.

.

6. Closing

Let's take a moment to think about something kind you could do for your Kindness pal today.
You can close your eyes if you want to. **Wait.**
Ask*: Who has an idea already of what you might do?* **Invite a few answers.**
You might say*: Thanks for a great class, everyone!*
Ring a bell or chime if you have one.

———————————

Extension: *Peace of Mind Core Curriculum for Grades 1 & 2*: Lesson 23 Blooming Breaths

Bubble Breathing

Invite a deep breath in and when you breathe out,
imagine that you are blowing bubbles!

Draw your own picture of Bubble Breathing below.

Candle Breathing

Imagine you are blowing out the
candles on your birthday cake.
Take three slow deep breaths.

Lesson 7
Visualization

Slides 74-84

1. Introduction

You might say: *Today we are going to learn a different kind of mindfulness practice and review the one we learned last time. Instead of focusing on Mindful Breathing we're going to be using our imaginations to travel to a Peaceful Place. Then we'll share about our Peaceful Place with our Kindness Pal and if we have time we'll draw a picture of it.*

2. Mindful Moment

Choose the Mindfulness Helper and Review

Ask if anybody remembers how to do Candle Breathing.

Choose the Mindfulness Helper and have them lead Candle Breathing.

Remind them to say, *"Let's get into our mindful bodies. Let's close our eyes or look down (it's important not to require students to close their eyes). Let's do Candle Breathing."* **Practice** a few rounds of Candle Breathing.

Ring a bell or chime if you have one.

Ask if anybody remembers how to do the other practices you've been learning. Ask them to demonstrate briefly.

Learn a new mindfulness practice with Malachi called Visualization**. Watch the Video Try** Visualization with the class.

Discuss

Do you think Visualization would help you fall asleep? Could it be helpful at other times?

3. American Sign Language (ASL)

Today we're going to learn how to say "Peaceful" in ASL.
How do you feel in your body when you feel peaceful?

Choose a few volunteers to demonstrate what "peaceful" looks like.
Let's watch a video of one of the Peace of Mind students showing us how to sign "peaceful." **(the video is in the slides)**

ASL Practice
Have everyone try to say "peaceful" in ASL. Point out that the sign involves our faces, hand gestures and body motions. Ask them if the sign matches the way that they feel when they feel peaceful.

4. Kindness Pals

Assign New *Kindness Pals: "Okay it's time to get our new Kindness Pals! There's one important rule of Kindness Pals. Does anybody remember what it is? When I tell you who your Kindness Pal is I want you to say "Okay!" in a nice friendly way.*

Kindness Pal Activity
Okay when I say go you're going to find your Kindness Pal and take turns telling each other about what you visualized. What is in your peaceful place?

Share: Give the class a chance to share about their Peaceful Place.

5. Optional

Visualization Coloring Sheet and Peaceful Place Drawing Sheet.

6. Closing

Let's take a moment to think about something kind you could do for your Kindness pal today. You can close your eyes if you want to.
Wait.
Ask: *Who has an idea already of what you might do?* ***Invite a few answers.***
You might say: *Thanks for a great class, everyone!*
Ring a bell or chime if you have one.

Extension: *Peace of Mind Core Curriculum for Grades 1 & 2 - Lesson 19 Another visualization practice, p. 100*

Visualization

Imagine you are in a peaceful place.
Imagine what you would see, hear,
taste, smell and feel in that place.

Draw a picture of your
Peaceful Place

What did you see, hear, smell, taste, touch, and feel?

Lesson 8:
Gratefuls

Slides 85-96

1. Introduction

You might say: _Today we are going to learn another kind of mindfulness practice and review the one we learned last time. Today's practice is about Gratitude or the feeling of being thankful. We're going to spend some time with our new Kindness Pal sharing about things we are grateful or thankful for._

2. Mindful Moment

Choose the Mindfulness Helper and Review

Ask if anybody remembers how to do Visualization.

Choose the Mindfulness Helper and have them lead a brief Visualization practice. **Remind** them to say, "_Let's get into our mindful bodies. Let's close our eyes or look down._ (It's important not to require students to close their eyes). _Let's do Visualization._

Ring a bell or chime if you have one.

Ask if anybody remembers how to do one or two of the other practices we've been learning. Ask them to demonstrate briefly.

Learn a new mindfulness practice with Peyton called Gratefuls. **Watch the video.** The students can practice with Peyton during the video. You may want to pause the video to give them more time to think.

Discuss
What was Peyton grateful for? What did you think of?

3. American Sign Language (ASL)

Today we're going to learn how to say "worried" in ASL.
How do you feel in your body when you feel worried?

Choose a few volunteers to demonstrate what "worried" looks like.

Let's watch a video of one of the Peace of Mind students showing us how to sign "worried." **(the video is in the slides)**

ASL Practice

Have everyone try to say "worried" in ASL. Point out that the sign involves our faces, hand gestures and body motions. Ask them if the sign matches the way that they feel when they feel worried.

4. Kindness Pals

Assign New *Kindness Pals: Okay it's time to get our new Kindness Pals! There's one important rule of Kindness Pals. Does anybody remember what it is? When I tell you who your Kindness Pal is I want you to say "Okay!" in a nice friendly way.*

Kindness Pal Activity:

Okay when I say go you're going to find your Kindness Pal and share three things you are grateful for. Then you can do the Gratitude worksheets together. Go!

5. Optional

Gratitude Coloring Sheet. If you have time you could make Gratefuls Boxes out of shoeboxes or brown paper bags.

6. Closing

Let's take a moment to think about something kind you could do for your Kindness pal today. You can close your eyes if you want to.
Wait
 Ask *Who has an idea of what you might do?* **Invite a few answers.**
Thanks for a great class, everyone!
Ring a bell or chime if you have one.

Extension: *The Peace of Mind Core Curriculum for Grades 1 and 2 - Unit 2: Gratitude includes 4 full lessons on gratitude practice and the brain's negativity bias. P. 61.*

What would you put in your Gratefuls Box?

Draw or write your ideas below

Gratitude

Think of little things you are grateful for. Write them down and save them to read later.

| 38

Lesson 9
Make up Your Own Breath

**Slides 97-107**

1. Introduction

You might say: _Today we are going to learn another mindfulness breathing practice called Wave Breaths and review the one we learned last time. Then you and your Kindness Pal will get to make up your own Mindful Breaths._

2. Mindfulness Moment

Choose the Mindfulness Helper and Review

Ask if anybody remembers how to do Gratefuls.

Choose the Mindfulness helper and have them lead a brief Gratitude practice.

Remind them to say, _"Let's get into our mindful bodies. Let's close our eyes or look down (it's important not to require kids to close their eyes). Let's think of three things we are grateful for."_

Ring a bell or chime if you have one.

Ask if anybody remembers how to do the other practices you've been learning. Ask them to demonstrate briefly.

Learn a new mindfulness practice with Silvia called Wave Breaths. **Watch the video**

Discuss: _What did you notice is different about Silvia from the other kids we've learned from? (she's a real kid, not a cartoon!) Silvia is a real kid who loves mindfulness. She loves to make up her own ways of taking her deep breaths._

Ask: _Can you think of your own way to do Wave Breaths?"_

Invite a few kids to share their ideas and encourage the other kids to try them out.

3. American Sign Language (ASL)

Today we're going to learn how to say "Loved" in ASL.
How do you feel in your body when you feel loved?

Choose a few volunteers to demonstrate what "loved" looks like.

Let's watch a video of one of the Peace of Mind students showing us how to sign "loved." **(the video is in the slides)**

ASL Practice

Have everyone try to say "loved" in ASL. Point out that the sign involves our faces, hand gestures and body motions. Ask them if the sign matches the way that they feel when they feel loved.

4. Kindness Pals

Assign New Kindness Pals: *Okay it's time to get our new Kindness Pals! There's one important rule of Kindness Pals. Does anybody remember what it is? When I tell you who your Kindness Pal is I want you to say "Okay!" in a nice friendly way.*

Kindness Pal Activity

Today you're going to make up your own way of doing Mindful Breathing. It can be anything like Jellyfish Breath, Fireworks Breaths, Baseball Breaths…anything that lets you do simple, slow movements with three deep breaths. Then you'll teach it to your new Kindness Pal and then you're going to draw it. You're going to make a picture just like the ones we've been coloring in Peace Class.

Invite students to draw their own mindful breathing practice on the attached worksheet.

5. Closing

Let's take a moment to think about something kind you could do for your Kindness pal today. You can close your eyes if you want to.
Wait.
Ask: *Who has an idea already of what you might do?* **Invite a few answers.**
Say: *Thanks for a great class, everyone!*
Ring a bell or chime if you have one.

———————

Extension: *Peace of Mind Core Curriculum for Grades 1 & 2: Lesson 14: Noticing Sensations. Help students practice a new kind of mindfulness exercise to notice what is happening in their bodies. P. 80.*

Create Your Own
Mindful Breathing Practice!

My Mindful Breathing Practice is called:

_____

Lesson 10
Sergio Sees the Good

Slides 108-124

NOTE: For this lesson you will need some small paper cups and marbles, beans, beads, or something small; enough for every Kindness Pal Pair to have about 10.

1. Introduction

You might say: Today's lesson will be a little different. I'm going to ask the Mindfulness Helper to choose one of the mindfulness practices we've learned and then we're going to listen to a story. We're going to learn about something called the Negativity Bias, learn how to say "I feel in ASL", and then we're going to do a fun activity with our Kindness Pals.

2. Mindful Moment

Choose today's practice.

Choose Mindfulness Helper. **Let the mindfulness helper choose** and help you to lead a mindfulness practice from all the practices you have learned so far.

Remind them to say, *"Let's get into our mindful bodies. Let's close our eyes or look down (it's important not to require students to close their eyes). Let's (fill in with chosen practice)….."* **Do** the practice.

Ring a bell or chime if you have one.

Invite a few kids to share their ideas and encourage the other kids to try them out.

3. American Sign Language (ASL)

Today we're going to learn how to say "I feel" in ASL. Then we can start to say "I feel happy or I feel sad, etc."

Let's watch a video of one of the Peace of Mind students showing us how to sign "I feel." **(the video is in the slides)**

ASL Practice

Have everyone try to say "I feel" in ASL. Then try adding some of the feeling words you've learned so far.

Read the book or watch the video of Sergio Sees the Good (8 mins) OR if you don't have time you can watch this 4 minute video Marleigh Sees the Good.

Discuss

- *Do you remember what each marble represents?*

- Since the marbles are probably all the same size you might ask whether all of the things that Sergio (or Marleigh) remembered had the same "weight" or "size". *Is waking up in a nice warm bed the same as hearing a funny joke?*

- *Do we sometimes forget about those big things and Invite them for granted?*

- *Have you ever had a day that was totally ruined? Looking back, do you think that was really true?*

- *Sergio's mom (or Marleigh's mom) explained why our brains have the Negativity Bias. Do you remember what she said?*

- *Do you think our Negativity Bias helps us in any way?* (Cactus example)

- *Does our Negativity Bias hurt us in any way?*

4. Kindness Pals

Assign New Kindness Pals

Okay it's time to get our new Kindness Pals! There's one important rule of Kindness Pals. Does anybody remember what it is? When I tell you who your Kindness Pal is I want you to say "Okay!" in a nice friendly way.

Kindness Pal Activity

Play the Marble Game.

Directions:

- Give each pair of Kindness Pals 3 paper cups and about ten marbles or other small objects. One cup is the "good" cup, one is the "bad" cup, and the other cup holds the small objects.

- Have them take turns.

- One student starts to recount their day to the other student.

- The student who is listening puts the marbles in the good or bad cups based on what the other student shares.

- The sharing student identifies what is good and what is bad (not the student putting the marbles in the cup).

- Have students notice how many marbles are in each cup when all 10 have been used: what kind of day has it really been so far for that student?

- Then they pour the marbles out and switch.

> **AUTHOR'S NOTE:** *It's important to remind students that bad things sometimes happen and we're not trying to pretend that they don't. But our brains don't need help remembering those things. Our brains <u>do</u> need help remembering the good things, especially the little ones. So taming the Negativity Bias is a good way of helping us to see our lives as they really are - the good and the bad and not just the bad.*

5. Optional

Work on Sergio's Scales Coloring Sheet with their Kindness Pals

6. Closing

Let's take a moment to think about something kind you could do for your Kindness pal today. You can close your eyes if you want to.

Wait.

Ask*: Who has an idea already of what you might do?* **Invite a few answers.**

Say*: Thanks for a great class, everyone!*

Ring a bell or chime if you have one.

Extension: *See the back pages in the book Sergio Sees the Good for more about the Negativity Bias and additional gratitude related activities.*

Peace of Mind®

Sergio's Scale

good   bad

Share with your Kindness Pal all the little things that
happened today and draw a marble on the good
side or the bad side for each thing you remember.

Lesson 11
Rosie's Brain

Slides 125-148

1. Introduction

You might say: *Today I'm going to ask the Mindfulness Helper to choose one of the mindfulness practices we've learned, we'll learn a new ASL sign, and then we're going to listen to a story about our brains. Then you're going to spend a little time with your Kindness Pals finding out how much you have in common.*

2. Mindful Moment

Choose Mindfulness Helper.**Let the mindfulness helper choose** and help you to lead a mindfulness practice from all the practices you have learned so far.

Remind them to say, "*Let's get into our mindful bodies. Let's close our eyes or look down (it's important not to require students to close their eyes). Let's (fill in with chosen practice) ….."* **Do** the Practice.

Ring a bell or chime if you have one.

3. American Sign Language (ASL)

Today we're going to learn how to say "Frustrated" in ASL.
How do you feel in your body when you feel frustrated?

Choose a few volunteers to demonstrate what "frustrated" looks like.

Let's watch a video of one of the Peace of Mind students showing us how to sign "frustrated." **(the video is in the slides)**

ASL Practice
Have everyone try to say "frustrated" in ASL.

Read the book or watch the video of Watch Rosie's Brain OR if you don't have time you can watch this 4 min video called **Marleigh's Brain.**

Discuss:
- *Why was Rosie angry?*
- *What did her Amygdala (Amy) want her to do?*

- *Was Amy's idea (smashing the piano) a good one?*

- *How did her Hippocampus (Miss Pickles) help her?*

- *How did her PFC help her?*

- *Can you think of another way to solve Rosie's (or Marleigh's) problem?*

- *What parts of your brain do you think you used to answer these questions?*

4. Kindness Pals

Assign New Kindness Pals

Kindness Pal Activity: *When I say "Go!" you're going to find your Kindness Pal and then I'm going to give you 30 seconds to find out how many things you have in common - how many things are the same about you. You can ask each other about foods you like, animals, colors, books, movies, toys, whatever!*

Who thinks they have the most things in common? Have everyone share one thing that they had in common with their Kindness Pal.

5. Optional

Brain Coloring Sheet

6. Closing

Let's take a moment to think about something kind you could do for your Kindness pal today. You can close your eyes if you want to.
Wait.
Ask: *Who has an idea already of what you might do?* **Invite a few answers.**
Say: *Thanks for a great class, everyone!* **Ring** a bell or chime if you have one.

_____

Extension: *The Peace of Mind Core Curriculum for Grades 1 & 2: Unit 4 Brain on Science includes 5 interactive lessons to help students learn more about their amygdala, hippocampus and prefrontal cortex and how to put this knowledge to work in their lives. P. 104*

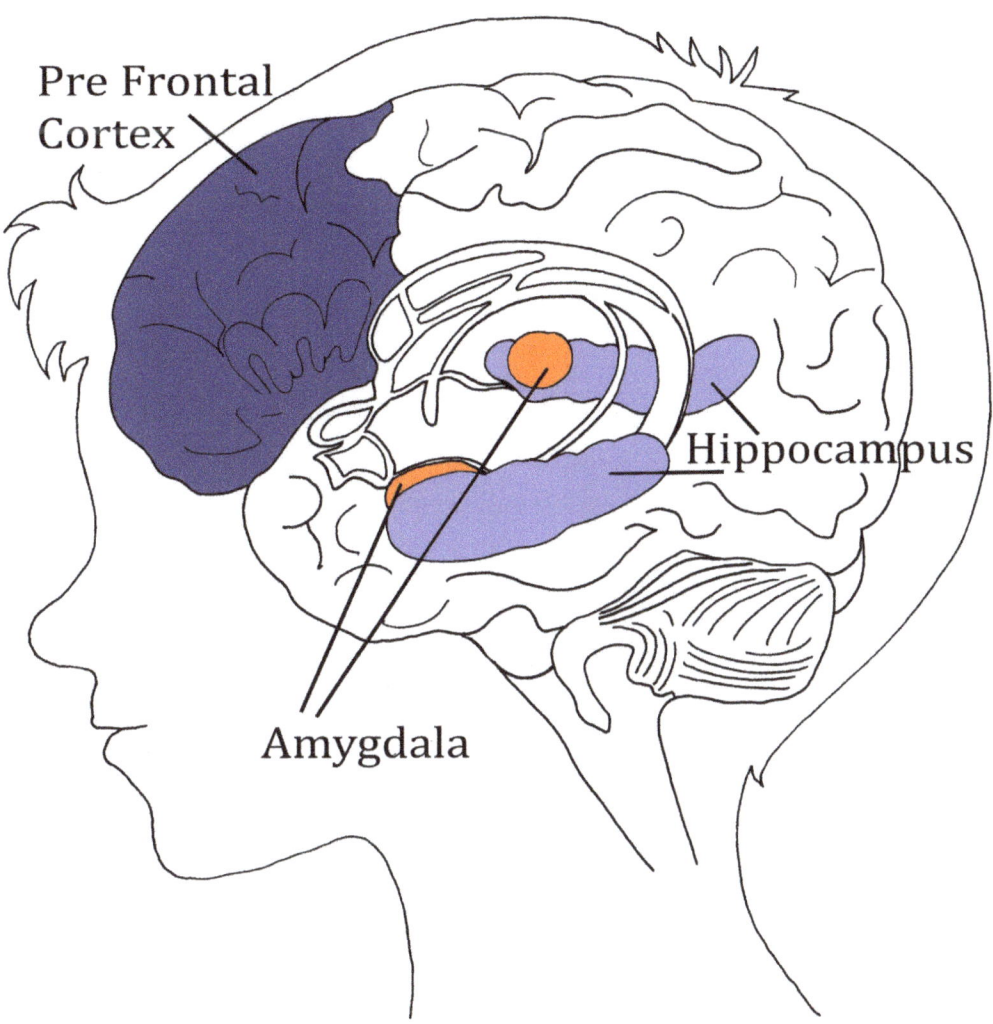

Pre Frontal Cortex

Hippocampus

Amygdala

Lesson 12
Daisy and Cactus: What is a conflict?

Slides 138-148

1. Introduction

You might say: *Today we're going to do our mindfulness practice and learn a new ASL sign. Then we're going to talk about conflict and see how two friends, Daisy and Cactus, solve a problem they are having.*

2. Mindful Moment

Have students choose a mindfulness practice for today.

Choose Mindfulness Helper.

Remind them to say, *"Let's get into our mindful bodies. Let's close our eyes or look down (it's important not to require students to close their eyes). Let's (fill in with chosen practice)….."* **Do** the practice.

Ring a bell or chime if you have one.

2. **American Sign Language (ASL)**

Today we're going to learn how to say "excited" in ASL.

How do you feel in your body when you feel excited?

Choose a few volunteers to demonstrate what "excited" looks like.

Let's watch a video of one of the Peace of Mind students showing us how to sign "excited." **(the video is in the Slides)**

ASL Practice

Have everyone try to say "excited" in ASL. Does the sign for "excited" match the way your body feels when you feel excited?

3. Conflict Resolution

Introduce the word "conflict."

You might say: *Today we are going to learn a new word. Has anybody ever heard the*

word conflict before? Does anybody have a guess about what it means?

Invite a few answers.

A conflict can be any kind of small problem. Maybe you are having a playdate, and you want to play outside, but your friend wants to play inside. Or maybe you want to play with your brother but he is busy doing his homework. Conflicts can stay small or they can get bigger.

Introduce the story

You might say: *Today we are going to act out a story about two best friends who have a conflict. Their names are Daisy and Cactus. I need two volunteers to act out the story.*

The volunteers will try to pretend that they are doing what their characters are doing. The rest of us are going to be paying close attention. First, I want you to raise your hand if you think you know what their conflict is about.

Keep paying attention. Each time you notice one of the characters getting mad or angry or making the problem bigger I want you to point up. If you notice that one of them is getting calmer and making things better I want you to point down.

Act out the story

Choose two actors to be Daisy and Cactus and ask them to act out the story (see next page) as you read it. If they feel comfortable, they can repeat their character's lines in addition to pantomiming the actions. Or they can act out the story without speaking.

Daisy and Cactus
by Linda Ryden

Once upon a time there were two friends named Daisy and Cactus. They did everything together. They even had a garden together. They dug holes in the garden together. They planted seeds in their garden together. They waited for the sunshine together. They watered their little plants together. They sang to their little plants together. And together they picked their flowers and vegetables when they were ready. They always worked together and they always shared. Well, almost always....

One day when they were out picking their flowers, Daisy saw the most beautiful rose. It was pink and white and had lots of soft petals. She picked the rose and held it up to her nose to smell it. She said, "Oh how beautiful! This rose makes me so happy!" When Cactus saw that Daisy had the rose, he felt angry. He had been watching that rose all week. He had even given it some extra water. He had planned to pick it and put it in a special vase. And now Daisy had it. He felt his angry feelings all the way in his belly. His face felt hot, he started breathing faster, and his hands balled up into little fists. He wanted the rose so badly that he tried to grab it away from Daisy.

"Give me my rose!" he shouted. When he grabbed the rose from Daisy he suddenly felt a sharp stinging pain in his fingers. "Ouch! The thorns stung my hand!" Now he was really, really angry so he threw the rose down on the ground and stomped on it with his feet.

When Daisy saw the smashed up rose on the ground she felt angry. "You're so mean, Cactus!" she shouted. "You ruined my beautiful rose!" And she curled up in a ball and cried.

When Cactus saw Daisy crying he felt awful. He really wanted the rose but he didn't want his friend to be so sad. He took five deep breaths until he felt his anger start to get smaller. Then he quickly ran back into the garden and found another rose. This one was yellow and smelled like sunshine. He brought it over to Daisy and said, "I'm sorry I took your rose and smashed it. I was so angry."

Daisy took a deep breath as she smelled the yellow rose. "That's okay," she said. "I'm sorry I yelled at you. I guess I flipped my lid too. And I'm sorry you got stung by the thorns. Are you okay?" Daisy wrapped a little piece of green grass around Cactus's finger. "Should we share this yellow rose?" said Cactus. And they went home and put the yellow rose in a beautiful vase.

The End

Discuss

- What was the conflict about?
- Why was Cactus so angry?
- How can you tell Cactus was angry?
- What did his face look like?
- What did his body look like?
- What part of Cactus's brain was in charge?
- Why was Daisy mad?
- Did getting mad make her cry?
- Do you ever feel like crying when you are angry?
- Did their conflict get bigger?
- What made it get bigger?
- Did they work out their conflict peacefully? How?

4. Kindness Pals

Assign New Kindness Pals

Kindness Pal Activity: Listening

Ask the class: Have you ever had a conflict with a friend?

When I say "Go!" you're going to find your Kindness Pal and tell him or her about it and then listen to their story. I'm going to ring a bell (in 30 seconds or a minute—whatever seems appropriate in the moment) and when you hear the bell, switch to listening to the other person.

5. Closing

Let's take a moment to think about something kind you could do for your Kindness pal today. You can close your eyes if you want to.

Wait.

Ask: *Who has an idea already of what you might do?* **Invite a few answers.**

You might say: *Thanks for a great class, everyone!* **Ring** a bell or chime if you have one.

Lesson 13
Jack and Louise: Conflict Resolution Practice

Slides 149-159

1. Introduction

You might say: *Today we're going to do our mindfulness practice and learn a new ASL phrase. Then we're going to talk more about solving conflicts and see how two friends, Jack and Louise, solve a problem they are having.*

2. Mindful Moment

Have students choose a mindfulness practice for today.
Choose Mindfulness Helper.
Remind them to say, *"Let's get into our mindful bodies. Let's close our eyes or look down (it's important not to require students to close their eyes). Let's (fill in with chosen practice) ….."*
Ring a bell or chime if you have one.

3. American Sign Language (ASL)

You might say: *Today we're going to learn how to say "How are you feeling today?" in ASL. Then we'll be able to ask each other about how we are feeling and answer!*

Let's watch a video of some Peace of Mind students showing us how to sign "How are you feeling today?" **(the video is in the Slides)**

ASL Practice
Have everyone try to say "How are you feeling today?" in ASL.

4. Conflict Resolution

Introduce the lesson and review the parts of the brain.
You might say: *In the last lesson we've learned what a conflict is. Today we are going to learn a few ways to work out our conflicts peacefully. Let's review the three parts of the brain we learned from Rosie's Brain and what they do.*

Talk about conflicts
You might say: *Let's say that you and your brother both want a cookie but there is only one cookie in the cookie jar.*

Discuss

- How would you feel?

- What would your Amygdala tell you to do?

- What would happen if you listened to your Amygdala?

- What could you do instead (share, eat something else, let your brother have the cookie)?

- Does your Amygdala know how to work out conflicts peacefully?

- What part of your brain knows how to work out conflicts peacefully? (The PFC)

- *Do you remember how you can get your PFC in charge again when your amygdala takes over? (Take deep breaths)*

Read and Act out the story.

You might say: *I'd like two volunteers to act out a little story. Our volunteers are going to pretend to be brother and sister. They are going to act out the story that I am telling using their bodies and their faces. They can repeat their character's lines if they want to.*

The volunteers will try to pretend that they are doing what their characters are doing. The rest of us are going to be paying close attention. First, I want you to raise your hand if you think you know what their conflict is about.

Keep paying attention. Each time you notice one of the characters getting mad or angry or making the problem bigger I want you to point up. If you notice that one of them is getting calmer and making things better I want you to point down.

Read the following story.

Allow time for the children to act out the activities and emotions you are describing.

The Story of Louise and Jack
By Linda Ryden

Louise and Jack are brother and sister. Usually they get along really well. They like to ride bikes, they like to swim, and they like to read. (Ask the class to come up with other activities Jack and Louise like to do and have the actors act out their ideas.)

Today they have been very busy and now they are tired… and hungry. They walk into their kitchen and reach into the cookie jar and they discover, gasp!, that there is only one cookie left! Oh no! Louise is very angry and says to Jack, "This is my cookie, let it go!"

Jack says, "No! This is my cookie! You let go!" They both grab onto the cookie and pull it back and forth between them.

Suddenly, Louise says, "Oh no! We are having a conflict!"

Jack says "You're right. Let's put the cookie down and Invite some deep breaths." They both Invite some nice, deep breaths. Feeling a little calmer, Jack says, "I'm sorry, Louise."

Louise says, "I'm sorry too, Jack. Do you want to share the cookie?" Jack says "Sure!" and splits the cookie in half. Then they happily eat the cookie together.

The End

Discuss
Ask: *Who can tell me what Jack and Louise did to work out their conflict?*
Invite a few answers.
You might say: *That's right, they decided to share the cookie.*
Ask: *Can you think of any other ways that Jack and Louise could have worked out their conflict?*

5. Kindness Pals

Assign New Kindness Pals

Kindness Pal Activity: Jack and Louise Worksheet
You might say: *These pictures are like a comic book version of the story we just acted out. The pictures start when the conflict starts.*

Directions:

- You and your Kindness pal are going to work together to put them in the right order.

- You'll put numbers on each drawing from 1 to 8 putting them in the order in which they happened in the skit.

- When we're done we'll go over the Worksheet all together and see how we did.

If you have time, act out the story again with a different solution.
When they are done then you can go over the answers together.

> *NOTE: Make sure that your students understand why it's so important that the mindful breathing comes before apologizing and working out the conflict. Remind them that people don't usually feel like apologizing when they are angry, but once they can calm down people often feel sorry about whatever they did or said that made the conflict escalate.*

6. Closing

Let's take a moment to think about something kind you could do for your Kindness pal today. You can close your eyes if you want to. **Wait.**
Ask: *Who has an idea already of what you might do?* ***Invite a few answers.***
Say: Thanks for a great class, everyone! **Ring** a bell or chime if you have one.

The Cookie Conflict
Put the pictures in order

Lesson 14
Henry is Kind

Slides 160-171

1. Introduction

You might say: *Today we're going to do our mindfulness practice and learn a new ASL word. Then we're going to talk about kindness and listen to a story about Henry, a boy around your age who didn't think he was kind at all until his friends helped him out.*

2. Mindful Moment

You might say: *Today we are going to learn a new kind of mindfulness practice called Heartfulness.* **Watch Heartfulness Video.**

Choose the Mindfulness helper. Help them to lead the class in heartfulness practice.

Remind them to say, *"Let's get into our mindful bodies. Let's close our eyes or look down (it's important not to require students to close their eyes). Let's …*

Help mindfulness helper lead the Heartfulness practice.

Ring a bell or chime if you have one.

Ask: How did this practice make you feel?

3. American Sign Language (ASL)

You might say: *Today we're going to practice saying "How are you feeling today?" and learn how to say "hungry" in ASL.*

Rewatch the demonstration of how to say "how are you feeling today?" and then choose a few volunteers to try it. Then choose a few volunteers to demonstrate how to say "I feel happy."

After we learn how to say "hungry" we'll practice having a conversation in ASL!

Ask: *How do you feel in your body when you feel hungry?*

Choose a few volunteers to demonstrate what "hungry" looks like.

Let's watch a video of one of the Peace of Mind students showing us how to sign "hungry." **(the video is in the Slides)**

ASL Practice

Have everyone try to say "hungry" in ASL. *Does the sign for "hungry" match the way your body feels when you feel hungry?*

ASL feelings check-in:

You might say: *Now I'm going to tell you who your new Kindness Pal is and you are going to ask each other how you are feeling today and answer!*

4. Kindness Pals

Assign New Kindness Pals and do feelings check-in. Have them practice answering the question with all the feelings words they can remember in ASL.

Read the book or watch the video of Henry is Kind.

Discuss:

- What is Heartfulness?
- Who would you like to send kind thoughts to?
- Why do you think it was hard for Henry to think of something kind he did?
- Why do you think Henry said "Kindness is stupid?"
- Do you think he really meant it?
- What was he feeling when he said that?
- Have you ever said something you didn't mean when you were upset?
- Can you think of a kind thing that you could do today when you get home?
- Are there kind things that you do every day, like feed your cat?

Kindness Pal Activity:

Play Three Animals Game. You and your Kindness Pal try to think of three animals that start with the first letter of your name and then you try to do the same with the first letter of your Kindness Pal's name. Try the same thing with foods, colors, sports… Have the children share some of their answers if there is time.

5. Closing

Let's take a moment to think about something kind you could do for your Kindness pal today. You can close your eyes if you want to. **Wait.**

Ask*: Who has an idea already of what you might do?* ***Invite a few answers.***

Say*: Thanks for a great class, everyone!*

Ring a bell or chime if you have one.

———————————

Extension: *The Peace of MInd Core Curriculum for Grades 1 & 2, Lesson 30 for more on Heartfulness and compassion. Page 158. Lesson 31, Gratitude Cards page 161Heartfulness*

Heartfulness

Who did you think your kind thoughts about?
Draw or write about them below.

May you be happy.
May you be healthy and strong.
May you be peaceful.

|

Lesson 15
Kindness Chain

Slides 172-180

NOTE: watch this <u>video</u> if you want to see an example of this activity.

1. Choose Mindfulness Helper and help them lead Heartfulness.

Remind the Mindfulness Helper one last time to say, *"Let's get into our mindful bodies. Let's close our eyes or look down (it's important not to require students to close their eyes). Let's … Do the Heartfulness Practice.*
Ring a bell or chime if you have one.

2. American Sign Language (ASL)

Today we're going to keep practicing saying "How are you feeling today?" and learn how to say "thirsty" in ASL.

Choose a few volunteers to demonstrate a conversation in ASL asking each other "how are you feeling today?" and then answering "I feel happy or sad or scared or hungry" etc.

After we learn how to say "thirsty" we'll do a feelings check-in with our new Kindness Pals!

Ask: *How do you feel in your body when you feel thirsty?*

Choose a few volunteers to demonstrate what "thirsty" looks like.

Let's watch a video of one of the Peace of Mind students showing us how to sign "thirsty." **(the video is in the Slides)**

ASL Practice
Have everyone try to say "thirsty" in ASL. *Does the sign for thirsty match the way your body feels when you feel thirsty?*

3. Kindness Pals Part 1

Assign New Kindness Pals and do feelings check-in. Have them practice answering the question with all the feelings words they can remember in ASL. Remind them that these are our last Kindness Pals.

ASL feelings check-in

You might say: *Now I'm going to tell you who your new Kindness Pal is and you are going to ask each other how you are feeling today and answer!*

Whole Group Activity: Kindness Chain

You might say: *This is our last Peace of Mind class and so it's a great time to show some kindness to each other. Today we are going to make a Kindness Chain. The first step is to gather into a circle.*

We are going to go around the circle and I'd like you to say something kind about the person sitting to your right. For example, I might say, "Cheryl, you are an awesome friend."

Cheryl might say "Thanks!" and then turn to the person on her right and say, "Harry, you are really good at building things."

And we'll go around the circle like that. Every once in a while when we play this game somebody's mind goes blank and they can't think of anything to say—even if they are sitting next to their best friend! If that happens to you, don't worry. Just say, "I need some help," and I will choose a volunteer to say something kind about that person. Then we'll continue going around the circle. When we're done, we'll go around the circle in the other direction.

This is a chance to use the power of our words to make people feel really good so let's try hard to take it seriously and make sure that everybody feels good. Ready to start?

4. Kindness Pals Part 2

Ask the students to move to sit next to your Kindness Pal. Prompt them to share how it felt to have someone say something kind about them. How did it feel to say something kind to someone else?

5. Closing:

This is our last class together. I hope that you enjoyed learning more about mindfulness, kindness, and how to work out our conflicts peacefully. The world needs lots of kind, mindful people. Now you have some tools to help you go out into the world and make it a more peaceful place. I hope you will!

Thank you so much!

About Linda Ryden, Author

Linda Ryden is the author of seven mindfulness-based children's books published by Cherry Lake Publishing and Peace of Mind Inc. Linda is the founder and Creative Director of Peace of Mind Inc. and creator of the Peace of Mind Program and author of the Peace of Mind Curriculum Series, a cutting-edge combination of mindfulness-based social-emotional learning, conflict resolution and social justice for Early Childhood through Middle School.Linda served as the full-time Peace Teacher at Lafayette Elementary School, Washington DC's largest public elementary school from 2003 to 2023, teaching Peace of Mind classes to more than 700 students every week.

Linda's work has been featured in The Washington Post, Washingtonian Magazine, Washington Parent, Washington Family, Teaching Tolerance, and Edutopia, among others. Linda was a keynote speaker at the National Network of State Teachers of the Year conference and a featured speaker at the National Education Association Foundation Symposium, and has received a Commendation for Educational Innovation from the DC Board of Education.

Linda lives in Washington D.C. with her husband Jeremiah Cohen, owner of Bullfrog Bagels, and their dog Phoebe.

In that small but growing band of peace educators, Linda Ryden stands out. The glistening ideas and stories in these pages are sure to open minds and stir hearts, in much the way that has been happening all these years with the children in her classrooms.

— Colman McCarthy, Founder of The Center for Teaching Peace

Bibliography

Bradshaw, C. P. (2015). Translating research to practice in bullying prevention. American Psychologist, 70 (4), 322-332.

Breeding, K., & Harrison, J. (2007). Connected and Respected: Lessons from the Resolving Conflict Creatively Program. Cambridge, Mass.: Educators for Social Responsibility.

Durlak, J. A., Weissberg, R. P., Dymnicki, A. B., Taylor, R. D. & Schellinger, K. B. (2011). The impact of enhancing students' social and emotional learning: A meta-analysis of school-based universal interventions. Child Development, 82(1): 405–432.

Hanson, R. (2015). Hardwiring Happiness. Random House USA.

Jennings, P. (2015). Mindfulness for teachers: Simple skills for peace and productivity in the classroom. The Norton Series on the Social Neuroscience of Education.

Jennings, P. A. (2019). The Trauma-Sensitive Classroom: Building Resilience with Compassionate Teaching. New York: W.W. Norton & Company.

Lantieri, Linda. "How SEL and Mindfulness Can Work Together." Greater Good. April 7, 2015. Accessed September 28, 2015. http://greatergood.berkeley.edu/article/item/how_social_emotional_learning_and_mindfulness_can_work_together.

Learning Heroes, Developing Life Skills in Children: A Road Map for Communicating with Parents, https://bealearninghero.org/parent-mindsets/ September 2018

O'Brennan, L., & Bradshaw, C. (2013). School Climate: A Research Brief. A report prepared for the National Education Association, Washington, DC.

Rechtschaffen, D., & Kabat-Zinn PhD, J. (2014). The Way of Mindful Education: Cultivating Well-being in Teachers and Students. Norton Books in Education. Schonert-Reichl, K. A., & Lawlor, M. S. (2010). The effects of a mindfulness-based education program on pre-and early adolescents' well-being and social and emotional competence. Mindfulness, 1(3), 137-151.

Schonert-Reichl, K. A., Oberle, E., Lawlor, M. S., Abbott, D., Thomson, K., Oberlander, T. F., & Diamond, A. (2015). Enhancing cognitive and social–emotional development through a simple-to-administer mindfulness-based school program for elementary school children: A randomized controlled trial. Developmental Psychology, 51(1), 52-66.

Seppala, E., Simon-Thomas, E., Brown, S. L., Worline, M. C., Cameron, C. D., & Doty, J. R. (2017). The Oxford Handbook of Compassion Science. New York, NY: Oxford University Press.

Siegel, D. J., & Bryson, T. P. (2012). The Whole-Brain Child. London: Constable & Robinson.

Simmons, Dena (2019), Why We Can't Afford Whitewashed Social-Emotional Learning Retrieved from http://www.ascd.org/publications/newsletters/education_update/apr19/vol61/num04

Srinivasan, M. (2014). Teach, Breathe, Learn: Mindfulness in and out of the Classroom. Berkeley, CA: Parallax Press.

Treleaven, David (2018). Trauma-Sensitive Mindfulness: Practices for Safe and Transformative Healing. New York: W. W. Norton & Company.

Weare, K. (2013). Developing mindfulness with children and young people: A review of the evidence and policy context. Journal of Children's Services, 8(2), 141-153.

Zoogman, S., Goldberg, S.B., Hoyt, W.T., & Miller, L. (2015). Mindfulness interventions with youth: A meta-analysis. Mindfulness, 6, 290 - 302.

Zenner, C., Hermleben-Kurz, S., & Walach, H. (2014). Mindfulness-based interventions in schools: A systematic review and meta-analysis. Frontiers in Psychology, 5, article 603.

Appreciation

Peace of Mind is based in our community, and we are so lucky to have the support and guidance and help of so many wonderful people. We are grateful to Mike Di Marco, Valentina Gabrielli and the teachers and staff of Horizons Greater Washington for inspiring us to create this curriculum and being our first pilot program in summer 2024. A fantastic group of educators in the DC area and beyond piloted the Flex Curriculum during the 24-25 school year and provided helpful feedback. This curriculum wouldn't exist without many wonderful friends of Peace of Mind including Kelly Gilstrap, Jillian Diesner, Jodi Ferrier, Elie Goldman, Jennifer Greene, our friends at Metamer Studios, and the students who helped to create the amazing ASL and mindfulness videos. As always, we are able to do what we do at Peace of Mind thanks to the support of very generous foundations and kind individual donors! Thank you!!

www.ingramcontent.com/pod-product-compliance
Lightning Source LLC
Chambersburg PA
CBHW040511150626
46551CB00030B/2502